AF270631

NFL Teams
DETROIT LIONS
KENNY ABDO
Fly!
An Imprint of Abdo Zoom
abdobooks.com

abdobooks.com

Published by Abdo Zoom, a division of ABDO, P.O. Box 398166, Minneapolis, Minnesota 55439. Copyright © 2022 by Abdo Consulting Group, Inc. International copyrights reserved in all countries. No part of this book may be reproduced in any form without written permission from the publisher. Fly!™ is a trademark and logo of Abdo Zoom.

Printed in China.
052021
092021

Photo Credits: AP Images, Getty Images, iStock, Shutterstock PREMIER
Production Contributors: Kenny Abdo, Jennie Forsberg, Grace Hansen
Design Contributors: Candice Keimig, Neil Klinepier

Library of Congress Control Number: 2020919488

Publisher's Cataloging-in-Publication Data

Names: Abdo, Kenny, author.
Title: Detroit Lions / by Kenny Abdo
Description: Minneapolis, Minnesota : Abdo Zoom, 2022 | Series: NFL teams | Includes online resources and index.
Identifiers: ISBN 9781098224615 (lib. bdg.) | ISBN 9781098225551 (ebook) | ISBN 9781098226022 (Read-to-Me ebook)
Subjects: LCSH: Detroit Lions (Football team)--Juvenile literature. | National Football League--Juvenile literature. | Football teams--Juvenile literature. | American football--Juvenile literature. | Professional sports--Juvenile literature.
Classification: DDC 796.33264--dc23

TABLE OF CONTENTS

Detroit Lions 4

Kick Off......................... 8

Team Recaps.................... 14

Hall of Fame 24

Glossary 30

Online Resources 31

Index 32

DETROIT LIONS

Spirited and strong, the Detroit Lions make their fans roar from the stands.

Despite many wins and playoff appearances, the Lions are one of the four NFL teams to have never played in a **Super Bowl**.

KICK OFF

The Lions started out as an independent pro team in 1929. They were based in Ohio and they were known as the Portsmouth Spartans. The team would join the NFL a year later.

In 1932, the Spartans played in
the first NFL playoff game. The
Spartans lost to the Chicago Bears
9-0. But the game was such a
success that the NFL decided to
repeat it.

George A. Richards bought the team in 1934. He moved the team to Detroit and gave it a new name. The Lions won their first NFL **championship** the next year!

TEAM RECAPS

In the 1950s, the Lions won the NFL **championship** three times! They made it to the playoffs in 1970 and 1982, but they lost both times. Things were looking up when the Lions won their division in 1983.

The Lions went on to win their division in 1991. It was one of their best seasons since 1970! The Lions won their division in 1993, too!

The 2000s were a dark decade. The Lions never made the playoffs. The 2011 season looked brighter. Matthew Stafford became the fourth **quarterback** in NFL history to throw more than 5,000 yards in a season. The Lions finished the 2014 season 11-5, its best record in 23 years.

STAFFORD
9

The 2019 season started off strong with a 2-0-1 record, but things would go south from there. Stafford broke his backbone in week 9. The Lions finished the season 3-12-1.

The Lions improved on their 2019 season with a 5-11 record in 2020. It would be their last season with Coach Matt Patricia. Fans hope new leadership and a fresh start will bring a brighter future!

HALL OF FAME

Dick Lane played six seasons with the Lions. During that time, he had 21 **interceptions** for 272 yards! Lane was called to the **Pro Bowl** three times. In 1974, Lane joined the Pro Football Hall of Fame.

Barry Sanders was named **Rookie** of the Year in 1989 and **Most Valuable Player (MVP)** in 1997. He was the first running back to rush for more than 1,000 yards in ten straight seasons. Sanders was **inducted** into the Pro Football Hall of Fame in 2004.

Matthew Stafford became the youngest **quarterback** to throw five or more touchdowns in a single game. In 2015, he reached 25,000 passing yards faster than any other player in NFL history.

GLOSSARY

championship – a game held to find a first-place winner.

induct – to admit someone as a member of an organization.

interception – when a player catches a pass that was meant for the other team's player.

MVP – short for "most valuable player," an award given in sports to a player who has performed the best in a game or series.

Pro Bowl – a game played once a year between two teams comprised of the NFL's all-stars.

quarterback (QB) – the player on the offensive team that directs teammates in their play.

rookie – a first-year player in a professional sport.

Super Bowl – the NFL championship game, played once a year.

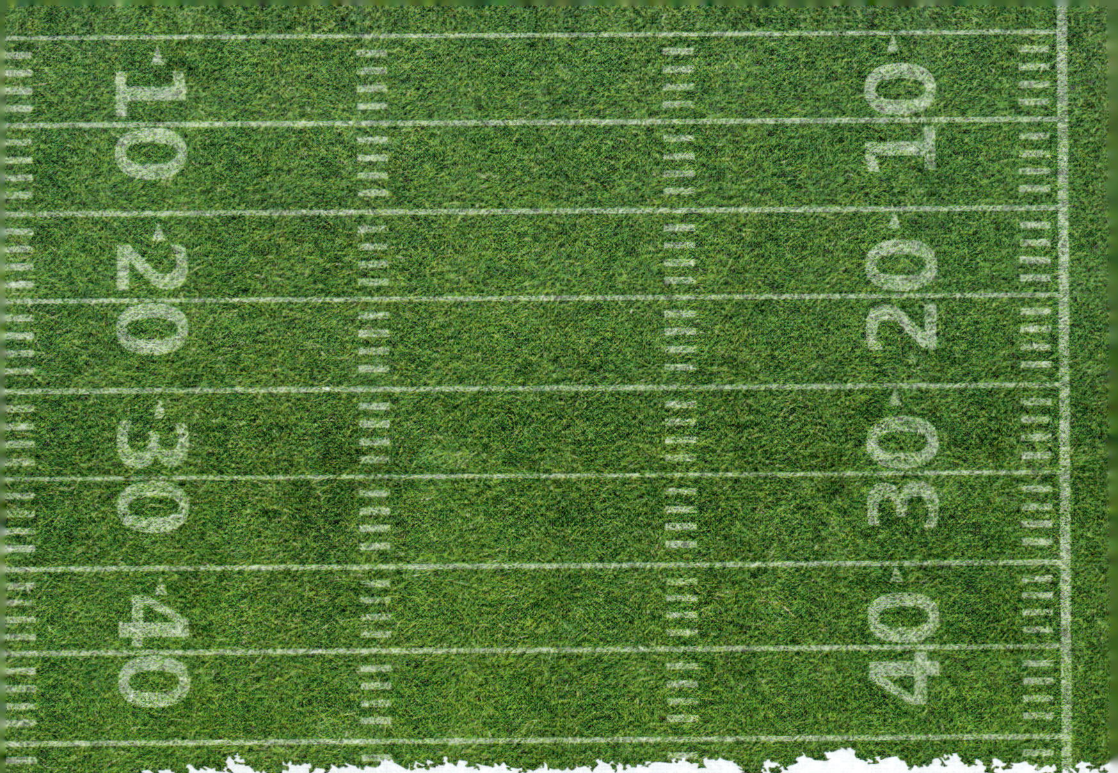

ONLINE RESOURCES

To learn more about the Detroit Lions, please visit **abdobooklinks.com** or scan this QR code. These links are routinely monitored and updated to provide the most current information available.

INDEX

Bears (team) 10

championships 10, 13, 15, 17

Lane, Dick 25

Ohio 8

Patricia, Matt 23

Pro Bowl 25

Richards, George A. 13

Sanders, Barry 26

Spartans (team) 8, 10

Stafford, Matthew 18, 20, 28

Super Bowl 7